FOUNDATIONS OF MACROECONOMICS

Integration Theory, Policy, and Practice

Ryan Bitstone

TOC

ISBN: 9781807650889

Published by TPSA Publishing

Acknowledgments

I would like to express my appreciation to a few of the many people to whom I am indebted for help in writing this book and getting it into print. First and foremost, I want to thank my wife Prema Popat, who spent many hours on short notice reading and critiquing the book in its entirety and—to my great benefit—sparing no criticism where it was needed. Next, my thanks go to Theodore Webb III, who helped me by researching the literature, working up spread sheets, and preparing the graphs and who caught many of my mistakes, typographical and otherwise. My colleague, Frank Conte, graduate assistant, Jonis Shehu, and intern, Matthew Dougherty provided valuable assistance in making final edits. Scott Isenberg, Executive Editor at Business Expert Press offered both patience and encouragement as I labored through the manuscript. Philip Romero and Jeffrey Edwards, Economics Co-Editors, provided many helpful suggestions, along with their patience and encouragement. Finally, my thanks to colleague Alison Kelly, whose prodding got me to refocus on this project after many years of hesitation and neglect. The legions of students whose questions and comments helped me organize my thinking are among the people too numerous to be mentioned by name. My thanks go to them, as well.

CHAPTER 1

Introduction

Macroeconomics is the study of the economy as a whole—as distinguished from microeconomics, which is the study of individual consumers, firms, industries, and markets. Microeconomics focuses on the individual economic decision maker (or *agent*) without attempting to take into account the full range of interactions that take place between one decision maker and another. Thus, for example, a study of the excise tax on cigarettes would consider the effect of that tax on the demand for cigarettes, but would not attempt to account for the effects of that tax on the demand for watermelon and the feedback effects on the demand for cigarettes.

When we do macroeconomics, we don't focus on cigarettes or watermelon. But we do focus on the interactions between large aggregates such as gross domestic product (GDP) and the markets for labor and capital. Indeed, we cannot do macroeconomics unless we break the economy into certain, broad constituent sectors and then study how they interact. At the heart of the question of how these sectors interact are the conditions that must prevail so that self-interested decisions of the individual economic agents who interact across these sectors will operate to their mutual advantage.

An economic system is one in which buyers and sellers coordinate their activities through a combination of market and government institutions. For the most part, and throughout the developed world, it is the market on which these individuals mainly rely for the coordination of their activities. There is, to be sure, a great deal of direction that comes from the government. Every country has a government that engages in its own transactions, and in some countries with mostly free economies these transactions account for a large fraction of economic activity. But the vast majority of transactions that take place around the world come about as a result of voluntary exchanges between buyers and sellers. The macroeconomic question is what policies are needed to make this system work effectively and what policies are called for when the system breaks down—as it surely can and will from time to time.

The possibility of system breakdown gives a second meaning to macroeconomics. Indeed, the field came into being from a book called *The General Theory of Employment, Interest, and Money,* published by John Maynard Keynes in 1936, which was all about how the economic system in place at the time broke down and deteriorated into a worldwide depression (Keynes 1936). Keynes did not use the word macroeconomics—that came later.[1] But he did set the stage for a formal theory of the economy in which wage and price adjustments that normally keep the economy at *full employment* (a term on which we elaborate below) fail and leave the economy in a state that calls for government intervention in the form of expansive monetary and fiscal policy. Government policies aimed at correcting the failure of an economic system to achieve full employment are frequently referred to as *stabilization policies*, connoting the idea that it is the job of the government to stabilize the economy at a level that brings about full employment.

From this Keynesian perspective, the distinction is between conditions that require no intervention by the government for the economy to function well (given that there will always be government interventions such as taxes and welfare benefits that affect the performance of the economy) and conditions that call for government deficits or an expansive monetary policy, that is, stabilization policies. A substantial part of this book is aimed at showing that a badly performing economy might just as well call for government surpluses or a contractive monetary policy.

There are therefore two ways of looking at the study of macroeconomics: (1) as a study of broadly defined economic sectors and how they interact, and (2) as a study of the breakdown in the process by which these sectors interact. Both approaches characterize the study of macroeconomics, and both will apply here. We are interested in the interactions between component parts of the economy under what we will call long-run or classical conditions *and* also in identifying the appropriate policy response when the decentralized price system breaks down and the economy falls into a period of subpar performance, that is, a recession or depression. In practice, such periods are referred to as the *short run*, even if they can last for many years, and call for a particular set of remedies that have to do with manipulating aggregate demand and supply. This is in contrast to the *long run*, when the (mostly) unregulated price system performs normally and the emphasis is on aggregate supply.

One respect in which this book differs from others has to do with the contention here that policy makers have to determine not only when the price system has broken down and thus when there is a case for the application of government stabilization measures, but also just *how* that system broke down and just what kind of intervention—expansive or contractive—is called for. Oddly for the many volumes of thought that the Keynesian revolution (and it was a revolution) produced, the debate since Keynes wrote the *General Theory* has been mostly over the simple question whether Keynes was right in his diagnosis of system failure and, if he was right, whether his offered remedies would work or not.

There wasn't a lot of debate over either question well into the 1960s. Most economists believed that Keynes was right on both counts. As Keynes saw it, his job was to debunk a *classical* tradition according to which observed deviations of economic activity from some normal state are self-correcting. The idea that a depressed economy would automatically right itself—insofar as anyone actually believed that at the time—had been rendered indefensible by the prolonged and severe economic downturn that began in 1929 and was at its height when Keynes published his book.

Beginning in the late 1960s, however, a counterrevolution was launched that challenged Keynes's ideas. This counterrevolution spawned a *new classical* economics, which argued that Keynes's remedies for a failing economy were likely to be ineffectual and unnecessary. This school of thought succeeded in stripping Keynes of much of his intellectual authority, at least until the recession that began in December 2007 and whose effects still linger today. It is safe to say that, until the downturn, the exponents of the new classical economics and their allies from various sub branches of this line of thinking carried the day.

I will state upfront that I subscribe to this new classical school, insofar as I think that it has much to say about improving both short-run and long-run economic performance, especially through tax and welfare reform.

Thus, the first eight chapters of this book are focused on explicating a *classical* world, in which the economy is performing normally (which is to say, it hasn't broken down owing to imbalances between aggregate supply and demand) and will respond positively to incentive-producing tax changes. The remaining chapters consider policies that are appropriate for correcting protracted periods of low employment.

I do not believe that protracted periods of low employment are a thing of the past (especially in the light of recent economic events) or that Keynes's prescriptions for righting a slumping economy are always wrong. What I do believe is that, while Keynes's prescriptions are sometimes right, they can also be just the opposite of what is called for.

A line of theorizing that emerged in the 1970s provides the basis for this assertion (Barro and Grossman 1976). The conclusion to which that line of theorizing leads is that the remedy for a sustained downturn might be government intervention through *contractive* monetary and fiscal policy. The intellectual foundations for this possibility have been in place for decades although much ignored.

Keynes's core idea was that a sudden, unanticipated fall in the demand for goods could create a state of affairs in which the economy would sink into a long-lasting slump. This fall in demand could come from various sources. (The fact that the U.S. money supply shrank by about a third during the Great Depression certainly suggests that a fall in aggregate demand was a principal cause of that downturn.) If a downturn occurs because of a fall in aggregate demand that came about because of monetary contraction, falling exports, a housing crisis, a related financial crisis, or any other such cause or combination of causes, then the obvious remedy is for the government to increase demand through expansive monetary and fiscal policy.

While there are differing views on how an unwanted decrease in demand could lead to economic collapse, the view adopted here is that it would happen because of a failure of wages and prices to adjust downward as needed to restore the demand for goods and labor. Unless prices and wages fall in tandem, firms cannot find enough buyers to buy their goods and workers cannot find enough employers to use their services. Failing a downward, parallel adjustment in prices and wages, there would emerge an excess supply of both goods and labor and a necessity for the government to restore aggregate demand through the adoption of expansive monetary and fiscal policies. Keynes saw this as the cure for the downturn in the midst of which he wrote his book.

The new classical response has been to argue that expansive monetary and fiscal policies will fail in their purpose once they are known, since individual economic agents will adjust their behavior in such a way as to defeat the purpose for which the policies are implemented. (Chapters 9 and 10 explore this possibility.) A collateral proposition is that the government should focus its attention not on the demand side but on the supply side of the economy, where it can improve the performance of the economy by reducing distortions in economic activity, particularly in the form of taxes.

The ordinary way of putting the distinction between Keynesian and new classical thinking is to recognize two states in which the economy can exist. One state—the classical state—represents the long run in which markets clear through appropriate price and wage adjustments and in which improvements in tax policy and other policies can yield benefits in the form of certain efficiency gains. (In fact, I give a lot of attention to this state.) The other state—the Keynesian state—represents the short run, when price and wage rigidities prevent markets from clearing and give rise to a fall in the demand for goods and labor. The trick is to recognize which state the economy is in and to apply the appropriate remedies.

In an article entitled "The Economy Needs More Spending Now," economist Alan S. Blinder offers exactly this characterization of the long-run and short-run distinction (Blinder 2013). "Poor economic policy," he argues, stems, among other things, from "the failure to distinguish between the short-run and the long-run effects of particular policies."

In the short run, Blinder says, "deficit reduction slows growth by cutting the economy's total spending." This is to be contrasted with the long run, during which deficits can lead to higher interest rates and reduced investment. "Long-run growth," Blinder writes, "is supply-determined. It depends on an economy's ability to produce more goods and services from one year to the next." The long run is all about utilizing "inputs more efficiently" to get the greatest attainable output.

In the short-run, however, output is demand determined. The big question is how much of the country's productive capacity is used. And that depends on the strength of demand—the willingness of businesses, consumers, foreign customers and governments to buy what American businesses are able to produce. (Blinder 2013)

Two Views of the Short Run

By the above argument, the short-run problem arises when the supply of goods and labor exceeds demand: The quantity of labor services demanded by firms is less than the quantity workers want to provide, and the quantity of goods demanded by consumers is less than the quantity firms want to provide.

What Blinder ignores, however, is an equally plausible short-run problem that arises when demand exceeds supply. The economy can suffer a downturn in production and employment because workers offer fewer labor services than firms want to hire and because firms offer fewer goods than consumers want to buy. Chapter 9 will show how both scenarios—generalized excess supply and generalized excess demand—are consistent with short-run economic decline.

Keynesians emphasize the scenario in which supply exceeds demand and in which prices and wages fail to adjust downward. That is why Blinder characterizes short-run unemployment as a demand-side problem: If the economy is suffering a protracted bout of low employment and production, it must be because aggregate demand is too low relative to aggregate supply, requiring a cure in the form of government policies, for example, deficits that will boost aggregate demand.

This, however, ignores the possibility that short-run low employment can present its own supply-side problem. This would occur because prices and wages failed to adjust *upwards*, as they should in response to an increase in aggregate demand, in order to bring aggregate supply into line with aggregate demand. This is often referred to as a case of *repressed inflation*, a name that it gets from wartime experiences with price -controls. As we go forward, we will see that the same phenomenon can result not only from price controls, but also from a failure of the economy to generate wage and price increases that are needed to keep aggregate supply in line with aggregate demand.

I believe that this scenario can be better described as *repressed wages* than as repressed inflation. A repressed wages scenario could develop either because of failure on the part of employers to raise wages in line with rising prices or due to other factors that prevent wages from rising in tandem with prices as aggregate demand rises.

Once we admit the possibility of repressed wages, we have to consider the fact that a protracted downturn could be the result of too much, rather than too little, aggregate demand. There can be subnormal production and employment if either aggregate supply exceeds aggregate demand or aggregate demand exceeds aggregate supply. In any economic downturn, there are clues as to which it might be—excess supply or excess demand—but often there will also be evidence that supports either interpretation.

A Revised View of the Long Run

This book focuses on macroeconomic policy and therefore gives attention both to policies that are effective in the long-run normal times and to policies that are needed in the short-run abnormal times. From the foregoing discussion, it is clear that in order to conduct this inquiry, it will be necessary to clean up some terminological confusion. First, it turns out that what we have come to call the *supply-side* approach to macroeconomic policy is mislabeled. That's because there exists the possibility of a supply-side problem that has nothing to do with using inputs more efficiently, but rather stems from a supply shortfall brought about by the maladjustment of prices and wages.

Henceforth, we will simply refer to solutions aimed at increasing economic efficiency as classical solutions, since the classical model assumes away the possibility of sustained excess supply or excess demand. We will give a great deal of attention to how the government can expand the economy by employing classical solutions, particularly solutions of the kind that consist of reducing distortions in the price system brought about by taxes.

However, when there is a failure of prices and wages to adjust and therefore a protracted downturn in the economy, there is a case for non-classical solutions in the form of expansive or contractive monetary and fiscal policy, whichever may be called for. Then the need will be for a correct diagnosis of the problem (too little demand or too little supply) and the application of the appropriate remedies.

By looking at the problem in this manner, we undertake a radical departure from conventional books on macroeconomics. Authors traditionally take the approach taken by Blinder in his *Wall Street Journal* article. In this traditional approach, there is only one diagnosis to perform, which is to answer the question whether the moment is right for a *demand-side* or for misnamed *supply-side* remedies.

This book approaches the problem differently. Having renamed as the classical approach what Blinder and many others call the supply-side approach, we first examine the economy under classical assumptions and consider the policies that are available to improve economic efficiency and through which to increase what we will call *long-run aggregate supply*. We next consider whether non-classical remedies—expansive or contractive monetary and fiscal policy—are called for.

In order to avoid terminological confusion, the book will recognize a distinction between two kinds of economic subperformance: (1) short-run (though, possibly protracted) subperformance brought about by imbalances between *aggregate* supply and demand and (2) long-run subperformance brought about by imbalances between *individual* supply and demand in the markets for labor and capital. In discussing the first kind of subperformance, we will distinguish between imbalances attributable to excess aggregate supply (the Keynesian scenario) and imbalances attributable to excess aggregate demand (the repressed wages scenario). In discussing the second kind of subperformance, we will characterize the problem as one that stems from government-imposed distortions in the price system.

The Great Contraction of 2007–2009 appears to have resulted from a Keynesian-type reduction in aggregate demand. In Chapter 12, we see evidence that the weakness of the ensuing recovery was attributable to a failure on the part of the government to adopt a sufficiently expansive policy response. Yet the evidence is not unambiguous. Given the distortions in the price system created by safety-net measures that took place concurrently with the downturn, it is possible that a contractive policy was called for. These competing explanations exemplify the difficulty policy makers encounter in their efforts to hit upon the correct response to an economic downturn.

Organization of the Book

First, a word of warning. This book is not going to be useful if the reader is unwilling to wade through some math and graphics. It is intended to be accessible to anyone who can remember his high school algebra. Such calculus as there is appears in an appendix and in footnotes. Yet the book is not for light reading during train or air travel. Better to enjoy the movie than to tackle this project. I hope, of course, that many readers will not be deterred and will wade through to the end.

Why all the math? The reason is that, without the math, the reader, to be blunt, will continue to be vulnerable to the great amount of folklore that continues to misinform just about everyone's understanding of the topic—and this, I am sorry to say, includes some distinguished macroeconomists. The math notwithstanding, the book should serve as a principal or supplementary text for Intermediate and Master's level courses in macroeconomics.

The book can be divided into six principal topics: (i) macro preliminaries (Chapters 1 and 2), (ii) micro foundations (Chapters 3 and 4), (iii) supply and demand for labor and capital (Chapters 5 and 6), (iv) fiscal and tax policy (Chapters 7 and 8), (v) competing theories of persistent unemployment (Chapters 9 and 10), and (iv) recent evidence and conclusions (Chapters 11 to 13).

It is hoped that the reader of this book will come away from it with a solid understanding of the micro foundations of macroeconomic analysis and, from that understanding, acquire a more sophisticated appreciation of the role of tax and fiscal policy in macroeconomic policy analysis. It is also hoped that he or she will come away from it with an understanding of how economic systems can slump into a protracted downturn and how, in forging the appropriate policy response to that downturn, it is important to diagnose correctly the cause of the downturn.

The book offers, as the title suggests, an integrative approach to its subject. Ever since Keynes's work, there has been tension between Keynesian and classical elements of macroeconomic theory. The goal here is to integrate these elements into a more internally consistent approach to the subject matter. More generally, the goal is to integrate the short-run and the long-run elements of macroeconomic activity and policy so as to avoid the approach common to other books, which is to take the reader through a series of alternative, disjointed models that leave the reader puzzled about which model works best.

This is not at all to say that I have been able to create a window to the world through which all macroeconomic reality can be seen clearly. On the contrary, I close with the warning that the evidence may point to many, equally plausible explanations of economic activity and as many plausible government policy options.

Indeed, I foresee a new era macroeconomic policy and practice—one in which policy makers will have to make, at best, informed conjectures about how best to deal with periods of protracted low employment. Contrary to conventional wisdom on this matter, there will be the difficult problem of choosing between expansive or contractive monetary and fiscal policy.

As the reader will see, however, the book does not take some relativistic approach, according to which one policy is as good as another. A view much emphasized in the concluding chapters is that the government's capacity to alleviate short-run problems is enhanced by its willingness to reduce distortions in the price system that worsen economic conditions both in the long run and the short run. Keynes is often quoted as saying that "in the long run we are all dead." True as that is, during the short run, when we are still alive, there is much about the long run that matters for how well we live—and how good we are at making macroeconomic policy.

[1] According to macroeconomist Kevin Hoover, the first person to use the term was the Norwegian economist (and future Nobel laureate) Ragnar Frisch in a lecture given in 1931 (Hoover 2008, 332).

CHAPTER 2

Macro Measurements

There are numerous ways to assess the performance of the macroeconomy. Toward the beginning of every month, the U.S. Bureau of Labor Statistics provides estimates of what might be the most commonly cited measures of macroeconomic performance—the number of jobs created or lost and the unemployment rate of the preceding month. The attention given to these numbers reflects the Keynesian-inspired preoccupation with jobs or, more precisely, with the failure of the private sector to *create* enough jobs to eliminate the excess supply of labor brought about by a lack of aggregate demand.[1]

As fascinated as politicians and the public might be with the jobs numbers, there is a more comprehensive measure issued every calendar quarter, and that is the growth of real, inflation-adjusted gross domestic product (GDP) during the preceding quarter. Economists refer to this indicator to assess macroeconomic performance.

GDP is the market value of final goods and services produced within a country over a year's time. Although it is the most commonly used measure of macroeconomic performance across the globe, GDP has come in for criticism in recent years as a macroeconomic indicator.

In his book, *Gross National Happiness*, Arthur C. Brooks claims that it is happiness that matters and that happiness has little to do with GDP but depends more on the nation's commitment to spiritual and family values.

The astronomical rises in American GDP reflect the fact that, as a nation, we are creating huge amounts of value—we are the most successful nation on earth. Yet ... happiness *doesn't* follow GDP growth over time. In the United States, our gross national happiness has remained essentially static for the past three decades. (Brooks 2008, 124–25; emphasis original) In 2008, President Nicholas Sarkozy of France commissioned a group of scholars to produce a report in which they would identify "the limits of GDP as an indicator of economic performance and social progress" -(Stiglitz, Sen and Fitoussi 2010, 2). A key finding was "that the time is ripe for our measurement system to *shift emphasis from measuring economic -production to measuring people's well-being*" (Stiglitz, Sen and Fitoussi 2010, 10; emphasis original). Alternative measures of well-being include consumption and household income, household wealth, the distribution of income and wealth, and nonmarket services that households provide for themselves (Stiglitz, Sen, and Fitoussi 2010, 1, 10–14). The shift from the production of goods to the production of services and the growing importance of services provided by the government make it imperative to reexamine what amounts to an increasingly antiquated method of measuring macroeconomic performance, or so the authors claim.

Crocodiles and GDP

A few years ago, I spent a week in Ghana, where I witnessed poverty of the kind that would jar any American. One day, I was eating lunch at a restaurant that my travel companion and I chose because it was built over a pond infested with crocodiles. (You don't get that eating at McDonald's in the United States.) As I ate, I happened to see two boys go down to that pond to fetch water, possibly for their mother's laundry. As I watched, I prayed that the crocodiles were too busy eating morsels tossed to them from the restaurant customers to attack the boys. And I thought of my own grandsons whose mother wouldn't let her children near the shallow end of the baby pool without all kinds of floating gear attached.

I relate this story to point out that it means something to say that the GDP per capita of the United States is about 32 times the GDP per capita of Ghana. We need comparisons like that because anecdotes about crocodiles are not enough to make economic policies. We need some way to track the difference it makes for individual living standards for government to implement policies that are intended to increase what we call *real* GDP (discussed in the next section). The question is not whether a single number will do but just what number best represents what it is that we are trying to measure. GDP is still that number.

This book, therefore, focuses on GDP and does so unashamedly. Yes, it is easy to cite examples of how GDP provides a misleading measure of economic performance and indeed, happiness. The destruction of the World Trade Center added billions of dollars to GDP in the form of construction costs for the new tower. Automobile accidents increase GDP by requiring the services of ambulances, doctors, car repair shops, and lawyers. Hard as it is to believe, the royalties paid to rap performers add to GDP. Drug deals that take place in the underground economy go uncounted. But these anomalies do not undermine the importance of measuring economic activity that does take place and, as puzzling as it often seems, in response to consumer demand. There is no conflict between the broad policy of increasing real GDP growth and the importance of discouraging terrorist attacks, traffic accidents, and loud, unpleasant noise masqueraded as music.

The problem with critiques such as those offered by Brooks and by the Sarkozy commission is that they make perfect sense without providing a useful alternative to GDP as a measure of economic performance. "Well-being is multidimensional," say the authors of the Sarkozy report (Stiglitz, Sen, and Fitoussi 2010, 15). Well, yes, but that's just the problem. Once we expand the measurement of economic performance to encompass indicators such as "political voice and governance" and "social connections and relationships," any hope of identifying policy changes that rather clearly improve or worsen macroeconomic performance is lost. To muse about social connections is to drift off into speculations about matters best left to social psychologists.

Nominal versus Real GDP

Let's consider a country that has two goods, A and B, which are produced over a span of two years. Table 2.1 provides data on the quantity of each good produced and the price at which it is sold each year. We see that \$60.00 (= \$1.00 × 60) worth of good A was produced in year 1 and \$162.50 in year 2. Thus, in *nominal* dollars, production increased by 171 percent. But not all of this increase was *real*. The number of units produced rose by only 8.3 percent (from 60 to 65). The rest of the increase in nominal output was inflation—the rise in price from \$1.00 to \$2.50. Similarly, the production of good B, in nominal dollars, rose from \$140.00 to \$247.50. Part of this was real—the rise in output from 70 to 90 units—and part inflation—the rise in price from \$2.00 to \$2.75.

Table 2.1 Prices and quantities, years 1 and 2

	Year 1	**Year 2**

Price ($) of good		
A	**$1.00**	**$2.50**
B	**$2.00**	**$2.75**
Quantity of good		
A	60	65
B	70	90

The first row in Table 2.2 provides calculations of nominal GDP [symbolized by the Greek letter *Y* (psi, pronounced as "sigh")] for each of the two years. Nominal GDP equals the market price of each good multiplied by the quantity produced and summed over all goods.

CHAPTER 3

CHAPTER 3

Microeconomic Foundations of Macroeconomic Analysis

Macroeconomics cannot be fully understood without a clear appreciation of its microeconomic foundations. While macroeconomic models often focus on aggregates such as total output, employment, and inflation, these aggregates are ultimately the result of millions of individual decisions made by households and firms. Understanding how these decisions are formed, coordinated, and sometimes distorted is essential to understanding how the economy behaves at the macro level.

At the heart of microeconomic behavior lies the concept of rational choice. Individuals are assumed to respond to incentives, weighing costs and benefits when making decisions about consumption, labor supply, and saving. Firms similarly respond to prices, wages, taxes, and regulations when deciding how much to produce, whom to hire, and where to invest. These decisions collectively shape aggregate supply and aggregate demand.

Households face trade-offs between consumption and leisure. When wages rise, work becomes more attractive relative to leisure, encouraging greater labor supply. Conversely, higher taxes on labor income reduce the reward from work and may discourage labor force participation. These responses matter greatly for macroeconomic outcomes, particularly employment and long-run growth. Policies that alter incentives at the individual level inevitably ripple through the entire economy.

Firms operate under constraints defined by technology, costs, and market conditions. Profit maximization leads firms to hire labor up to the point where the marginal product of labor equals the real wage. Capital investment decisions depend on interest rates, expected returns, and tax treatment. When governments impose regulations or taxes that distort these relationships, the result is often reduced efficiency and lower aggregate output.

Prices play a crucial coordinating role in market economies. They transmit information about scarcity and preferences, guiding resources to their most valued uses. When prices are allowed to adjust freely, markets tend to clear, meaning supply equals demand. However, when prices or wages are rigid—due to contracts, regulations, or institutional constraints—imbalances can persist, leading to unemployment or shortages.

Microeconomic foundations also help explain why policy interventions sometimes fail. If individuals anticipate policy changes, they may adjust their behavior in ways that offset the intended effects. For example, an anticipated increase in inflation may lead workers to demand higher wages, neutralizing expansionary monetary policy. This insight, central to new classical economics, underscores the importance of expectations in macroeconomic analysis.

In summary, macroeconomic outcomes emerge from microeconomic behavior. Policies that ignore incentives, expectations, and individual decision-making risk producing unintended consequences. A solid understanding of microeconomic foundations is therefore indispensable for effective macroeconomic policy design.

A deeper examination of microeconomic behavior reveals that incentives operate not only through explicit prices and wages, but also through institutional structures and social norms. Legal frameworks governing property rights, contract enforcement, and market entry significantly influence how individuals and firms respond to economic signals. When property rights are well defined and contracts are reliably enforced, individuals are more willing to engage in exchange, invest resources, and undertake entrepreneurial risk. Conversely, weak institutions increase uncertainty, discourage investment, and distort individual decision-making, ultimately impairing aggregate economic performance.

Transaction costs play an important role in shaping microeconomic outcomes. These costs include the time, effort, and resources required to find trading partners, negotiate contracts, and enforce agreements. In an idealized world of zero transaction costs, markets would function seamlessly and resources would flow effortlessly to their most productive uses. In reality, transaction costs are pervasive and can lead to market frictions that prevent efficient outcomes. These frictions help explain why firms exist, why markets are sometimes incomplete, and why government intervention may occasionally be justified to reduce inefficiencies.

Another critical microeconomic foundation of macroeconomic analysis lies in the role of information. Economic agents often make decisions under conditions of imperfect or asymmetric information. Consumers may lack full knowledge about product quality, workers may not know all available job opportunities, and firms may have limited information about future demand. Asymmetric information can lead to adverse selection and moral hazard, phenomena that distort market outcomes and affect macroeconomic variables such as employment, credit availability, and output growth.

Financial markets provide a clear illustration of how micro-level information problems can have macroeconomic consequences. Lenders must assess the riskiness of borrowers, while borrowers may have incentives to conceal unfavorable information. When information asymmetries become severe, credit markets can contract, even in the presence of profitable investment opportunities. Such contractions can amplify economic downturns by restricting access to capital, reducing investment, and increasing unemployment. Understanding these microeconomic mechanisms is essential for interpreting financial crises and their macroeconomic impact.

The concept of time also plays a central role in individual decision-making. Households and firms routinely make intertemporal choices, trading off present consumption or investment against future benefits. Saving behavior reflects preferences over time, expectations about future income, and prevailing interest rates. When individuals anticipate higher future taxes or lower future income, they may increase current saving, reducing aggregate demand. Similarly, firms may postpone investment if future policy environments appear uncertain or unfavorable. These intertemporal decisions, aggregated across millions of agents, shape business cycles and long-term growth trajectories.

Behavioral considerations further enrich the microeconomic foundations of macroeconomics. While traditional models assume fully rational agents, empirical evidence suggests that individuals sometimes exhibit bounded rationality, relying on rules of thumb rather than optimizing behavior. Cognitive biases, such as loss aversion or overconfidence, can influence spending, saving, and investment decisions. Although these behaviors may appear minor at the individual level, their aggregate effects can be substantial, contributing to asset price bubbles, excessive risk-taking, or prolonged periods of economic pessimism.

Labor market behavior illustrates the interaction between rational incentives and institutional constraints. Workers choose whether to participate in the labor force based on wages, taxes, benefits, and personal preferences. Firms decide how many workers to hire based on productivity, labor costs, and expected demand. However, labor markets are embedded within legal and social institutions that influence wage-setting and employment relationships. Employment protection laws, collective bargaining arrangements, and social insurance systems can alter incentives in ways that affect employment levels and labor mobility.

Human capital investment represents another microeconomic foundation with profound macroeconomic implications. Individuals invest in education and training to enhance their productivity and earning potential. These investments depend on expected returns, access to financing, and institutional support. At the aggregate level, human capital accumulation drives productivity growth, innovation, and competitiveness. Policies that improve access to education and reduce barriers to skill acquisition can therefore yield long-term macroeconomic benefits.

Entrepreneurship serves as a critical link between micro-level incentives and macroeconomic performance.

Entrepreneurs identify opportunities, allocate resources, and introduce innovations that expand productive capacity. The decision to start a business depends on expected profits, regulatory burdens, access to capital, and tolerance for risk. Economies that foster entrepreneurial activity through clear rules, low entry barriers, and supportive institutions tend to experience higher growth and greater adaptability to economic change.

Microeconomic foundations also help clarify the limits of macroeconomic stabilization policies. When governments attempt to influence aggregate demand through fiscal or monetary measures, individual agents may respond in ways that dilute or offset policy effects. For example, temporary tax cuts may be saved rather than spent if households expect future tax increases. Similarly, firms may refrain from expanding production if they believe policy-induced demand increases are short-lived. These responses underscore the importance of credibility and policy design.

Price signals remain the primary mechanism through which decentralized decisions are coordinated in market economies. When prices reflect underlying scarcity and preferences, they guide resources efficiently. Distortions introduced by price controls, subsidies, or poorly designed regulations can obscure these signals, leading to misallocation. Shortages, surpluses, and reduced productivity often follow. Microeconomic analysis provides the tools needed to understand how such distortions arise and how they propagate through the economy.

In open economies, microeconomic decisions are influenced by international trade and capital flows. Firms choose whether to export or import based on relative prices and comparative advantage. Workers may face increased competition from foreign labor markets, while consumers benefit from a greater variety of goods at lower prices. Exchange rates, tariffs, and trade policies affect these decisions, with aggregate consequences for output, employment, and income distribution. Understanding these effects requires careful attention to individual incentives within a global context.

Ultimately, macroeconomic stability depends on the consistency between individual incentives and collective outcomes. When policies align private decision-making with social objectives, markets tend to function smoothly. When they do not, tensions arise that can manifest as unemployment, inflation, or slow growth. Microeconomic foundations provide a framework for diagnosing these tensions and evaluating alternative policy approaches.

By grounding macroeconomic analysis in individual behavior, economists gain a clearer understanding of how economies function and why they sometimes fail. Aggregate variables are not independent forces acting on passive agents; they are the emergent results of countless decisions made under specific incentives and constraints. Recognizing this reality is essential for developing policies that enhance efficiency, resilience, and long-term prosperity.

CHAPTER 4

CHAPTER 4

Expectations and Economic Behavior

Expectations play a central role in shaping economic outcomes. Households and firms do not make decisions based solely on current conditions; they also consider what they believe will happen in the future. These expectations influence consumption, investment, wage negotiations, and price-setting behavior, making them a critical component of modern macroeconomic theory.

One of the most influential developments in macroeconomics was the introduction of rational expectations. This concept holds that economic agents use all available information, including knowledge of government policies, to form expectations that are, on average, accurate. While individuals may make mistakes, these errors are not systematic. As a result, predictable policy actions may have little real effect on economic behavior.

Expectations affect consumption decisions through income forecasting. If households expect higher future income, they may increase current consumption, even if present income has not yet risen. Conversely, pessimistic expectations can lead to higher saving and reduced spending, dampening aggregate demand. Investment decisions are similarly forward-looking, relying heavily on expectations of future profitability.

Inflation expectations are particularly important. When workers and firms expect higher inflation, they adjust wage demands and prices accordingly. This can create self-fulfilling inflationary pressures. Central banks therefore devote significant effort to managing expectations through credible policy commitments and transparent communication.

The credibility of institutions matters greatly. When governments or central banks have a history of policy reversals or excessive intervention, their announcements may be discounted by the public. In contrast, credible commitments can stabilize expectations and reduce economic volatility. This insight has led to greater emphasis on rules-based policy frameworks rather than discretionary actions.

Expectations also help explain why short-run policy trade-offs may disappear in the long run. Attempts to reduce unemployment through unexpected inflation may succeed temporarily, but once expectations adjust, unemployment returns to its natural level while inflation remains higher. This principle challenges the effectiveness of activist stabilization policies.

Ultimately, expectations link present decisions to future outcomes. Any comprehensive macroeconomic analysis must account for how individuals interpret policy actions and economic signals. Ignoring expectations risks misunderstanding both the causes of economic fluctuations and the limits of policy intervention.

Expectations are formed through a continuous process of learning and adaptation. Economic agents observe past outcomes, interpret new information, and revise their beliefs accordingly. This adaptive process means that expectations are not static but evolve in response to policy changes, economic shocks, and institutional performance.

As a result, the effectiveness of macroeconomic policy depends not only on the policy itself, but also on how quickly and accurately expectations adjust to new conditions.

Information channels play a crucial role in shaping expectations. Media coverage, official statistics, central bank announcements, and political discourse all contribute to how individuals perceive the economic environment. When information is clear, consistent, and credible, expectations tend to converge, reducing uncertainty. When information is conflicting or unreliable, expectations may diverge, increasing volatility in consumption, investment, and financial markets.

Forward-looking behavior is particularly evident in financial markets, where asset prices reflect collective expectations about future economic conditions. Stock prices incorporate anticipated profits, interest rates, and growth prospects, while bond yields reflect expectations about inflation and monetary policy. Sudden shifts in expectations can therefore trigger rapid changes in asset prices, even in the absence of immediate changes in underlying economic fundamentals. These expectation-driven movements can amplify business cycles and transmit shocks across the economy.

The role of expectations is also central to the conduct of monetary policy. Modern central banks recognize that influencing expectations may be as important as adjusting policy instruments themselves. Forward guidance, which involves communicating future policy intentions, aims to shape expectations about interest rates and inflation. When credible, such guidance can affect economic behavior today by altering long-term interest rates and borrowing decisions.

However, the effectiveness of expectation management depends critically on institutional credibility. If economic agents doubt a central bank's commitment to its stated objectives, forward guidance may fail to influence behavior. Repeated deviations from announced targets can undermine trust, making future communication less effective. This erosion of credibility can force policymakers to rely on more aggressive interventions, increasing the risk of unintended consequences.

Fiscal policy is likewise shaped by expectations. Government spending increases or tax cuts may have different effects depending on whether households view them as temporary or permanent. If individuals expect higher future taxes to offset current deficits, they may increase saving rather than consumption, reducing the stimulus effect. This phenomenon, often associated with Ricardian equivalence, highlights how expectations about future policy paths influence present economic outcomes.

Expectations also influence wage-setting and labor market dynamics. Workers negotiate wages based not only on current labor market conditions but also on expected inflation, productivity growth, and job security. Employers, in turn, set wages and hiring plans based on expectations about future demand and costs. Misaligned expectations between workers and firms can lead to wage rigidity, unemployment, or inflationary pressures.

In periods of economic instability, expectations can become unanchored. During recessions, pessimistic expectations may persist even after objective indicators begin to improve. This phenomenon, sometimes described as confidence-driven stagnation, can slow recovery by suppressing consumption and investment. Restoring confidence in such circumstances requires not only policy action but also credible signals that future conditions will improve.

Expectations are also shaped by historical experience. Economies that have experienced high inflation, financial crises, or policy instability often exhibit more cautious behavior long after conditions normalize. These legacy effects can influence saving patterns, risk tolerance, and trust in institutions. Understanding the historical context is therefore essential for interpreting expectation formation and its macroeconomic implications.

The interaction between expectations and uncertainty deserves special attention. While expectations reflect beliefs about likely outcomes, uncertainty refers to the degree of confidence individuals have in those beliefs. High uncertainty can dampen economic activity even when expectations are broadly optimistic. Firms may delay investment and hiring decisions, and households may postpone major purchases, leading to slower growth despite favorable forecasts.

Policy frameworks that reduce uncertainty can therefore have powerful stabilizing effects. Clear rules, transparent decision-making processes, and consistent enforcement help anchor expectations and encourage long-term planning. In contrast, frequent policy reversals or ambiguous commitments increase uncertainty, weakening the transmission of policy measures to real economic activity.

Expectations also play a role in shaping inflation dynamics beyond traditional demand pressures. If firms expect higher future costs, they may raise prices preemptively. Similarly, if workers anticipate rising prices, they may seek higher wages, reinforcing inflationary momentum. These expectation-driven processes highlight why inflation control requires more than short-term demand management.

From a theoretical perspective, expectations bridge the gap between microeconomic decision-making and macroeconomic outcomes. Individual beliefs about the future guide present choices, and the aggregation of these choices determines overall economic performance. This linkage underscores why macroeconomic models that ignore expectations often fail to predict real-world outcomes accurately.

The limits of policy intervention become clearer when expectations are taken seriously. Attempts to exploit short-run trade-offs between inflation and unemployment may fail if agents anticipate policy actions and adjust behavior accordingly. This insight has reshaped modern macroeconomic thinking, emphasizing credibility, rules, and long-term consistency over discretionary fine-tuning.

In conclusion, expectations are not a peripheral consideration but a central organizing principle of macroeconomic analysis. They influence nearly every aspect of economic behavior, from household consumption to financial market dynamics and policy effectiveness. A rigorous understanding of expectation formation and its consequences is essential for explaining economic fluctuations and for designing policies that achieve sustainable stability and growth.

CHAPTER 5

CHAPTER 5

Labor Markets and Employment Dynamics

The labor market is a central focus of macroeconomic analysis because employment is closely tied to economic well-being. Understanding how labor markets function, and why they sometimes fail to clear, is essential for diagnosing economic downturns and evaluating policy responses.

In a classical framework, wages adjust to equate labor supply and labor demand. When wages are flexible, any excess supply of labor leads to downward wage pressure, restoring equilibrium. Under these conditions, unemployment is largely voluntary, reflecting individual preferences rather than systemic failure.

In practice, however, wages are often rigid. Minimum wage laws, collective bargaining agreements, efficiency wages, and social norms can all prevent wages from adjusting downward. As a result, negative shocks to demand may translate into persistent unemployment rather than lower wages.

Efficiency wage theories suggest that firms may deliberately pay wages above market-clearing levels to boost productivity, reduce turnover, or attract higher-quality workers. While beneficial at the firm level, this practice can contribute to economy-wide unemployment by keeping wages artificially high.

Labor market policies also shape employment outcomes. Unemployment benefits provide income support but may reduce incentives to search for work if poorly designed.

Payroll taxes increase the cost of labor, discouraging hiring. Well-intentioned regulations can thus have unintended consequences.

Understanding labor market dynamics requires balancing efficiency with equity. Policymakers must weigh the benefits of worker protection against the costs of reduced employment. A macroeconomic framework grounded in labor market realities is essential for designing policies that promote both prosperity and social stability.

Labor markets are shaped not only by wages but also by a wide range of non-wage factors that influence both labor supply and labor demand. Working conditions, job security, opportunities for advancement, and workplace flexibility all affect individuals' decisions to participate in the labor force and to accept particular jobs. These factors help explain why labor markets do not always behave as simple price-clearing mechanisms and why unemployment can persist even in the absence of explicit wage rigidity.

Job search and matching processes introduce additional frictions into labor markets. Workers do not instantly find jobs that match their skills, and firms do not immediately locate suitable candidates. Time spent searching for employment, gathering information, and evaluating opportunities contributes to what economists refer to as frictional unemployment. Even in a healthy economy, some level of unemployment is unavoidable due to these matching frictions.

Structural unemployment arises when there is a mismatch between the skills workers possess and the skills demanded by employers. Technological change, globalization, and shifts in consumer preferences can render certain skills obsolete while increasing demand for others. Workers displaced from declining industries may face prolonged unemployment if retraining opportunities are limited or costly. At the macroeconomic level, structural mismatches can reduce potential output and slow economic growth.

Labor mobility plays a critical role in mitigating unemployment. Geographic mobility allows workers to move from regions with limited job opportunities to those with stronger labor demand. Occupational mobility enables workers to transition between industries or roles. Barriers to mobility, such as housing costs, licensing requirements, or social ties, can exacerbate unemployment by preventing labor from reallocating efficiently.

The role of institutions is particularly pronounced in labor markets. Employment protection legislation, while designed to safeguard workers, can increase the cost of hiring and firing, making firms more cautious about expanding their workforce. This caution may reduce job creation, particularly for young and inexperienced workers. The trade-off between job security and labor market flexibility is a recurring theme in labor market policy debates.

Unions influence wage-setting and employment conditions through collective bargaining. By negotiating higher wages and better benefits, unions can improve worker welfare. However, when negotiated wages exceed productivity levels, employment may decline. The macroeconomic impact of unions depends on the balance between wage gains, productivity effects, and labor market flexibility.

Demographic factors also shape labor market outcomes. Aging populations affect labor supply, potentially leading to labor shortages and increased fiscal pressure on social insurance systems. Changes in female labor force participation, immigration patterns, and educational attainment alter the composition of the workforce and influence overall employment dynamics.

Expectations, discussed in the previous chapter, play a significant role in labor markets as well. Firms base hiring decisions on expectations about future demand, costs, and regulatory environments. Workers' expectations about job prospects and wage growth influence their willingness to search for work or invest in additional skills. Pessimistic expectations can suppress hiring and prolong unemployment during economic downturns.

The interaction between labor markets and business cycles highlights the distinction between cyclical and structural unemployment. During recessions, job losses are often driven by reduced demand for goods and services. As demand recovers, employment typically rebounds. However, if recessions are prolonged or accompanied by structural changes, cyclical unemployment may evolve into structural unemployment, complicating recovery efforts.

Active labor market policies aim to address these challenges by improving job matching and skill acquisition. Training programs, job placement services, and wage subsidies seek to enhance employability and reduce unemployment duration. The effectiveness of such policies varies widely and depends on program design, targeting, and implementation.

Informal labor markets further complicate employment dynamics. In many economies, a significant share of employment occurs outside formal regulatory frameworks. Informal work may provide income opportunities when formal jobs are scarce, but it often lacks legal protections and social benefits. At the macroeconomic level, widespread informality can reduce tax revenues, distort labor statistics, and weaken social insurance systems.

Labor market dynamics also have important distributional consequences. Wage dispersion reflects differences in skills, experience, and bargaining power. Technological change has increased demand for high-skilled workers while reducing demand for routine tasks, contributing to wage inequality. Policymakers face the challenge of addressing inequality without undermining incentives for skill acquisition and productivity.

From a macroeconomic perspective, sustained employment growth depends on an environment that encourages job creation, skill development, and labor mobility. Stable macroeconomic conditions, predictable regulations, and policies that align incentives with productivity growth support healthy labor markets. Conversely, policies that distort labor costs or reduce flexibility can impede adjustment and slow recovery.

In evaluating labor market policies, it is essential to consider both short-term and long-term effects. Measures that protect existing jobs may reduce layoffs in the short run but discourage new hiring in the long run. Similarly, generous unemployment benefits may provide valuable income support while potentially extending unemployment durations if incentives are misaligned.

Ultimately, labor markets reflect a complex interaction of incentives, institutions, and expectations. A nuanced understanding of these dynamics is essential for designing policies that promote employment, productivity, and social cohesion. Macroeconomic analysis grounded in labor market realities provides the foundation for achieving sustainable and inclusive economic growth.

CHAPTER 6

CHAPTER 6

Capital Markets and Economic Growth

Capital accumulation is a key driver of long-term economic growth. Investments in physical capital, human capital, and technology expand productive capacity and raise living standards. Macroeconomic policy plays an important role in shaping the incentives for investment.

Interest rates coordinate saving and investment decisions. When interest rates are low, borrowing becomes cheaper, encouraging firms to invest. High interest rates, by contrast, discourage investment and may slow growth. Monetary policy thus influences capital formation through its effect on financial conditions.

Taxes on capital income affect the after-tax return on investment. High capital taxes can discourage saving and investment, leading to slower capital accumulation. Conversely, policies that promote investment through tax incentives or regulatory reform can enhance growth.

Uncertainty is a major deterrent to investment. Firms are less likely to commit resources when policy environments are unstable or unpredictable. Clear, consistent rules help reduce uncertainty and foster long-term planning.

Capital markets also facilitate risk-sharing and resource allocation. Efficient financial systems channel funds to their most productive uses, supporting innovation and entrepreneurship. Weak or distorted financial markets can misallocate capital, undermining growth.

Sustained economic growth depends on policies that encourage investment, innovation, and efficient capital allocation. Macroeconomic stability, credible institutions, and sound incentives form the foundation for long-term prosperity.

Capital accumulation encompasses more than the expansion of physical assets such as machinery, buildings, and infrastructure. It also includes investments in human capital and knowledge, which are essential for sustaining productivity growth in advanced economies. Education, training, and research enhance the ability of workers and firms to adopt new technologies and improve production processes. At the macroeconomic level, these investments raise potential output and increase an economy's capacity to generate income over time.

Technological progress interacts closely with capital markets. Innovations often require substantial upfront investment with uncertain returns, making access to financing critical. Well-functioning capital markets enable firms to fund research and development, scale successful innovations, and diffuse new technologies throughout the economy. When financial systems fail to allocate capital effectively, promising projects may go unfunded, slowing technological advancement and long-term growth.

The structure of financial markets influences how capital is allocated. Bank-based systems rely heavily on financial intermediaries to assess risk and monitor borrowers, while market-based systems emphasize securities markets and direct financing. Each structure has advantages and vulnerabilities. Bank-based systems may provide stability and long-term relationships, but they can also be prone to concentrated risk. Market-based systems promote transparency and diversification but may amplify volatility during periods of financial stress.

Financial intermediation reduces the costs associated with matching savers and investors. By pooling resources and spreading risk, intermediaries enable households to earn returns on savings while providing firms with access to capital. This process enhances overall economic efficiency. However, excessive risk-taking or weak regulation can undermine financial stability, leading to crises that disrupt investment and growth.

Expectations and confidence play a central role in capital market behavior. Investors base decisions on anticipated returns, policy environments, and macroeconomic conditions. When confidence is high, capital flows toward productive investments, supporting expansion. When confidence deteriorates, capital may retreat to safe assets, reducing investment and slowing growth. These shifts can occur rapidly, underscoring the sensitivity of capital markets to changes in sentiment.

The relationship between savings and investment is influenced by demographic trends. Aging populations may alter saving behavior, increasing demand for secure assets while reducing risk tolerance. Changes in population growth and workforce participation affect the availability of labor and the returns to capital. Policymakers must account for these demographic forces when designing strategies to promote sustainable growth.

International capital flows add another layer of complexity to capital markets. Open economies can attract foreign investment, supplementing domestic savings and supporting growth. At the same time, reliance on external financing exposes economies to global financial conditions and sudden reversals of capital flows. Managing openness while maintaining financial stability is a key challenge for policymakers.

Capital markets also influence income distribution. Returns to capital accrue disproportionately to those who own financial assets, potentially widening wealth inequality. While capital accumulation raises overall living standards, its distributional effects may generate social and political tensions. Balancing efficiency with equity requires careful policy design that promotes broad participation in the benefits of growth.

The role of government in capital markets is multifaceted. Public investment in infrastructure, education, and basic research complements private investment and can crowd in additional capital formation. At the same time, poorly targeted subsidies or excessive regulation may distort incentives and reduce efficiency. Effective public policy seeks to create an environment in which private investment can flourish while addressing market failures.

Macroeconomic stability is a prerequisite for healthy capital markets. High inflation, volatile exchange rates, and fiscal imbalances increase uncertainty and discourage long-term investment. Stable monetary and fiscal frameworks help anchor expectations and reduce risk premiums, lowering the cost of capital. This stability supports sustained investment and growth.

Financial crises illustrate the macroeconomic consequences of failures in capital markets. Excessive leverage, asset price bubbles, and weak oversight can culminate in sudden collapses that disrupt credit flows and reduce output.

Recovering from such crises often requires restoring confidence, recapitalizing financial institutions, and reforming regulatory frameworks. The long-term costs of financial instability highlight the importance of prudent capital market governance.

Capital allocation decisions are also influenced by environmental and social considerations. Increasing attention to sustainability has led investors to incorporate environmental, social, and governance factors into decision-making. These considerations can reshape investment patterns and influence long-term growth trajectories. Integrating sustainability with economic efficiency presents both challenges and opportunities for capital markets.

In the long run, economic growth depends on the alignment of incentives across households, firms, and financial institutions. Policies that encourage saving, reward productive investment, and foster innovation create a virtuous cycle of capital accumulation and growth. Conversely, policies that distort returns or increase uncertainty can hinder capital formation and reduce economic potential.

The interaction between capital markets and other sectors of the economy underscores the integrative nature of macroeconomic analysis. Labor markets, discussed in the previous chapter, influence the returns to capital through productivity and wage dynamics. Expectations, examined earlier, shape investment decisions and asset prices. Understanding these interconnections is essential for developing coherent economic policy.

Ultimately, capital markets serve as the engine of long-term economic growth by channeling resources toward their most productive uses. Their effectiveness depends on sound institutions, credible policies, and a stable macroeconomic environment. By fostering efficient capital allocation and supporting innovation, well-functioning capital markets lay the groundwork for rising living standards and enduring prosperity.

CONCLUSION

CONCLUSION

Integrating Theory and Policy

Macroeconomics is ultimately about understanding how complex systems of individual decisions produce collective outcomes. Throughout this book, we have emphasized the importance of integrating microeconomic foundations with macroeconomic analysis to achieve a coherent understanding of economic behavior.

Economic systems can perform remarkably well under the right conditions, coordinating decentralized decisions through prices and incentives. However, they are not immune to breakdowns. When prices and wages fail to adjust, or when policies distort incentives, economies can experience prolonged periods of underperformance.

Effective policy requires accurate diagnosis. Not all downturns are alike, and not all call for the same remedies. Expansionary policies may be appropriate in some circumstances, while contractionary measures may be needed in others. The challenge lies in recognizing the underlying causes of economic weakness.

This book has argued against one-size-fits-all solutions. Instead, it advocates a disciplined approach grounded in theory, evidence, and an appreciation of institutional realities. By integrating classical and non-classical perspectives, policymakers can better navigate the trade-offs inherent in economic management.

While uncertainty is unavoidable, informed conjecture is preferable to dogmatic adherence to outdated models. A deeper understanding of incentives, expectations, and market dynamics enhances our ability to design policies that promote stability, growth, and shared prosperity.

A central theme of this book has been the necessity of moving beyond rigid theoretical divisions and toward a more integrated framework for macroeconomic analysis. The long-standing separation between classical and non-classical approaches has often obscured rather than clarified the true sources of economic instability. By recognizing that economies operate under varying conditions, and that no single model applies universally, policymakers and analysts can develop more flexible and effective responses to economic challenges.

One of the key lessons is that economic outcomes cannot be divorced from the incentives faced by individuals and institutions. Policies that appear sound at the aggregate level may fail if they neglect how households, firms, and investors adjust their behavior in response to changing rules and expectations. Conversely, policies grounded in an understanding of microeconomic behavior are more likely to achieve their intended objectives and to do so with fewer unintended consequences.

The importance of expectations has emerged repeatedly throughout this analysis. Economic agents do not respond mechanically to policy interventions; they interpret signals, form beliefs about the future, and adjust their actions accordingly. When expectations are well anchored by credible institutions and consistent policy frameworks, economies tend to exhibit greater stability and resilience.

When expectations become unanchored, even well-intentioned policies may lose effectiveness.

This book has also emphasized the role of institutions in shaping economic performance. Markets do not function in a vacuum; they depend on legal frameworks, regulatory environments, and social norms that influence behavior. Strong institutions enhance trust, reduce transaction costs, and facilitate efficient coordination. Weak or inconsistent institutions increase uncertainty and undermine economic performance, often exacerbating cyclical fluctuations and slowing long-term growth.

A recurring challenge in macroeconomic policy is distinguishing between short-run disruptions and long-run structural problems. Short-run downturns may arise from temporary imbalances between aggregate supply and demand, calling for stabilization measures. Long-run underperformance, by contrast, often reflects deeper distortions in incentives, productivity, or capital allocation. Confusing these two sources of economic weakness can lead to inappropriate policy responses that worsen rather than alleviate problems.

The analysis presented here underscores the need for careful diagnosis before intervention. Expansionary fiscal or monetary policies can be powerful tools when economies suffer from insufficient demand, but they are not universally appropriate. In some circumstances, contractionary measures or structural reforms may be required to restore balance and improve performance. Effective policymaking depends on understanding which conditions prevail and responding accordingly.

Another important insight concerns the limits of government action. While public policy plays a crucial role in stabilizing economies and correcting market failures, it is not omnipotent. Attempts to fine-tune economic outcomes often encounter information constraints, political pressures, and unintended behavioral responses. Recognizing these limitations encourages humility and reinforces the value of rule-based frameworks that promote predictability and accountability.

The interaction between macroeconomic policy and long-term growth is particularly significant. Policies designed to address short-run fluctuations should not undermine the incentives that drive investment, innovation, and productivity growth. Sustainable prosperity requires an environment that rewards productive activity, encourages skill acquisition, and facilitates efficient capital allocation. Short-term gains achieved at the expense of long-term incentives may prove costly over time.

This book has argued that economic resilience depends on aligning short-run stabilization efforts with long-run efficiency objectives. Reducing distortions in labor markets, tax systems, and regulatory frameworks enhances the economy's capacity to adjust to shocks and to recover from downturns. Such reforms may not yield immediate political rewards, but they form the foundation for durable economic performance.

Globalization and technological change further complicate the policy landscape. Open economies are increasingly interconnected through trade, finance, and information flows. Shocks originating in one region can quickly propagate across borders, amplifying their impact. Policymakers must therefore consider both domestic conditions and global dynamics when designing economic strategies.

At the same time, globalization has heightened concerns about inequality and social cohesion. While economic growth raises overall living standards, its benefits are not always evenly distributed. Addressing distributional concerns without undermining efficiency represents one of the central challenges of modern macroeconomic policy. Policies that expand opportunity, enhance mobility, and support human capital development offer promising avenues for reconciling growth with equity.

The framework developed in this book rejects simplistic narratives that portray economic policy as a choice between unfettered markets and heavy-handed intervention. Instead, it recognizes the complementary roles of markets and institutions in shaping outcomes. Markets excel at coordinating decentralized decisions, while institutions provide the rules and safeguards that enable markets to function effectively.

As economic conditions evolve, so too must analytical frameworks and policy approaches. Relying on outdated models or ideological prescriptions risks misdiagnosing problems and applying ineffective remedies. Continuous evaluation, empirical testing, and openness to new evidence are essential for improving macroeconomic understanding and practice.

In closing, macroeconomics is best viewed as an evolving discipline rather than a settled body of doctrine. Its insights are most valuable when they are applied with care, contextual awareness, and respect for the complexity of economic systems. By integrating theory with empirical observation and institutional analysis, economists and policymakers can better navigate uncertainty and promote economic outcomes that enhance prosperity and well-being.

The ultimate objective of macroeconomic policy is not simply to manage aggregates, but to create conditions under which individuals and firms can make productive choices, adapt to change, and pursue opportunity. Achieving this objective requires sound incentives, credible institutions, and a willingness to learn from both success and failure. The integrative approach advanced in this book is intended as a step toward that goal.

www.ingramcontent.com/pod-product-compliance
Lightning Source LLC
LaVergne TN
LVHW022323200926
848481LV00004B/1404